A DAY AT THE RACES

with AUSTIN and KYLE PETTY

Aerial view
of Charlotte
Motor Speedway

To Dad and Mom,
for taking me to the races
E.C.M.

For their help and assistance, the author would like to thank: Brian Asack, Andy Belmont, Charlotte Motor Speedway, Jim Donnelly, Doyle Ford, Jane Gossage, Sue Kassirer, Brice King, Kate Klimo, the MELLO YELLO crew, Theresa Moseley, NASCAR, the Petty family, and Barbara Sullivan.

Cover photo by Cindy Karam
Charlotte Motor Speedway photo used with permission of Charlotte Motor Speedway

"Mello Yello" is a registered trademark of The Coca-Cola Company.

Library of Congress Cataloging-in-Publication Data:
Mott, Evelyn Clarke   A day at the races with Austin and Kyle Petty / story by Evelyn Clarke Mott ; photographs by Evelyn Clarke Mott and Brian Asack.
p.   cm.–(Random House pictureback)   Summary: Text and photographs follow champion driver Kyle Petty and his son during a day at the stock car races.
ISBN 0-679-83258-0 (pbk.) 1. Stock car racing–United States–Juvenile literature. 2. Fathers and sons–United States–Juvenile literature. 3. Petty, Kyle–Juvenile literature. [1. Stock car racing. 2. Petty, Kyle.] I. Asack, Brian, ill. II. Title.
GV1029.9.S74M68   1993 796.7'2'0973–dc20   92-10947

Manufactured in the United States of America 10 9 8 7 6 5 4 3 2 1

Caution—danger
on the track

One lap to go

Severe danger—stop the race

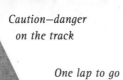

A DAY AT THE RACES

with *AUSTIN* and *KYLE PETTY*

Give way—faster car
behind

Story by **Evelyn Clarke Mott**
Photographs by **Evelyn Clarke Mott**
and **Brian Asack**

Finish

A Random House PICTUREBACK®

Make a pit stop
on the next lap

Go—start the race

76

Random House 🏠 New York

It was the day of the big stock-car race! Austin and his best friend, Brice, couldn't wait to see Austin's father, Kyle, race. Kyle Petty had been a race-car driver since long before Austin was born. So had Austin's grandfather—and even his great-grandfather!

"Hi, Dad!" said Austin when they arrived at the track. "Ready for the race?"

"Almost," Kyle said as he shook hands with Brice. "Good to see you, Brice. I'm glad there's time for Austin to show you around. Gary, my crew chief, is expecting you in the garage. I'll meet you in the trailer in an hour. Have fun!"

Austin took Brice into the noisy garage, where mechanics were busily working on the brightly painted cars.

"*Vrrrrooooom!*" went two long, snake-like hoses that helped take engine noise and fumes out of the garage.

Austin whistled loudly when he found his favorite car, the *Mello Yello* car. "This is my dad's car," he said to Brice.

From a distance *Mello Yello* looked like an everyday car, but up close it looked more like a spaceship.

On the dashboard were clockfaces that measured everything from speed and water temperature to oil pressure and the amount of gas in the tank. The strangest thing of all was the steering wheel. It sat upside down on the dashboard, leaving room for Kyle to climb into his seat.

Kyle's crew prepared to replace *Mello Yello*'s engine for the long 500-mile race. Standing underneath the hood, the mechanics disconnected the old engine from the car.

"Hi, guys," said Gary. "You're in for a treat. Watch this!"

Gary wheeled an engine hoist up to the car. He attached the engine to a chain and pushed down, hard, on a red lever. Up came the engine, out of the car and into the air.

After the crew had examined the old engine, they connected the new one to *Mello Yello*.

They tuned the new engine,

inspected the fuel tank,

and changed the rear sway bar, a bar that ties the left end of the car to the right end, to improve the way the car turns.

Meanwhile, a crewman was cutting pieces of plastic and attaching them to the trunk lid to raise the spoiler. Gary explained that a spoiler is like a wing and that a higher spoiler would hold the *Mello Yello* car's back down. That would help *Mello Yello* go faster on turns without slipping.

Next, Gary used a scale to measure the weight pressing down on the *Mello Yello* car's right wheels. He decided the *Mello Yello* car would turn faster with new springs and tires.

"Come on, guys," he said to Austin and Brice. "Let's pick up some tires."

Austin and Brice followed Gary to the tire stand. Workers were busily mounting and balancing tires for the race.

Gary took one set of tires back to *Mello Yello*. Two crewmen wheeled seven more sets over to the pit area, the place where *Mello Yello* would stop for gas or servicing during the race.

"Time to meet my dad, Brice!" said Austin. "Let's go!"

On the way to meet Kyle, Austin and Brice walked past a long line of giant tractor-trailers.

Brice liked the *Mello Yello* car's trailer best, with its red, green, and yellow jagged stripes.

Cabinets inside the trailer held parts, supplies, tools, and team uniforms.

An extra *Mello Yello* car was parked overhead.

Austin and Brice found Kyle putting on his racing clothes in the dressing room.

"Why do you wear those special clothes?" Brice asked.

"Safety," said Kyle. "Racing shoes protect my feet from too much heat, and this jumpsuit is made of material that can protect my body in case of a fire. Even my gloves, head sock, and underwear are fireproof."

"Cool," said Brice.

"Cool is the way I hope to stay." Kyle laughed. "See you later. It's time for me to join the lineup."

"Yay, Dad! Good luck!"
Austin gave his father a
high-five.

Kyle climbed through the *Mello Yello* car's window, because race cars don't have doors.

Kyle fastened his seat belt, attached the steering wheel,

slipped on a head sock, strapped on his helmet,

and put on his gloves. Kyle and Austin waved to one another.

Austin said good luck to his grandfather, Richard, who was also in the race.

A racing fan named Chubby howled what sounded like "Hello."

"Look at that hat!" Austin said. "I hope we don't have to sit behind *him*!"

Austin and Brice
found their seats just as
the loudspeaker boomed,
"Racers, start your engines!"

The roar of the cars and the cheers of the fans filled the stadium.

To help the race-cars' engines warm up, a pace car led the cars around the track. Its yellow lights flashed brightly.

CHARLOTTE

WINSTON POLE DAY
OCTOBER 2

CHARLOTTE
MOTOR
SPEEDWAY

ALL PRO
AUTO PARTS 300
OCTOBER 5

OFFICIAL PACE CAR

NASCAR

Swerving from side to side, the drivers scuffed and heated their tires to give their cars a better grip on the track.

After three laps, the pace car pulled off the track. A flagman waved the green flag to start the race.

"V-a-a-a-rooooooooooooom!" The colorful cars zoomed past with a thunderous roar.

Bumper to bumper, the cars raced at speeds of over 180 miles per hour. Smells of burning rubber and gasoline filled the air.

Mello Yello sped into fifth place.

Sounding like a swarm of angry bees, the cars buzzed past the grandstands again.

Kyle drove *Mello Yello* right up behind Car 7, and the two cars began drafting, or traveling close together at the same speed. By cutting through the wind as a pair, both cars were now going faster than they had on their own.

Suddenly a car bounced and spun out of control. Blue smoke streamed from the tires. Car parts flew every which way. Austin and Brice jumped to their feet.

"WHOA!!!" blared the loudspeaker. "We have a collision on the second turn—looks like Car 95."

Yellow lights went on all around the track.

The flagman waved the yellow flag, which meant DANGER! SLOW DOWN!

A fireman rushed to the accident.

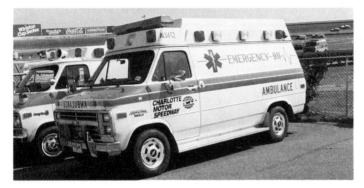

Other rescue workers and vehicles sped over and stood by. The crowd applauded when they heard that the driver was all right.

Car 95 was towed to its pit area.

The pace car returned. It slowly led the other cars until the workers had cleaned up the track. As soon as the pace car pulled off the track, the cars flew past the green flag. The race was on once again!

"V-a-a-a-rooooooooooooom!"
"Go, Dad!" shouted Austin.
The cars circled the track, over and over, in a rage of sound and color.

The crew waited as Gary radioed Kyle for a pit stop.

"The *Mello Yello* car's almost out of fuel," said Gary. "Time to pit!"

While the other cars kept racing, *Mello Yello* headed down to its pit area. Six crew workers jumped over the guardrail and sped into action. They changed tires, adjusted the chassis, added 22 gallons of gasoline, cleaned the windshield, and gave Kyle a cup of cold water—all in 14 seconds! *Mello Yello* roared back to the track.

Meanwhile, the pit crew threw the *Mello Yello* car's hot tires over the guardrail. A mechanic checked their temperatures with a pyrometer to find out if the tires had gripped the track properly. After racing, tire temperatures are usually over 220° Fahrenheit—hotter than boiling water!

The crew looked the tires over for any unusual marks to see if the car needed any adjustments.

After 300 laps, *Mello Yello* pulled into second place.

Soon *Mello Yello* was tailing the first-place car. The flagman waved the white flag, which meant one lap to go.

"Come on, Dad! You can do it!" yelled Austin.

"Go, Kyle! We want Kyle!" Brice shouted.

Mello Yello jerked to the left, sped up even more, and zoomed into first place.

Mello Yello streaked over the finish line.

The checkered flag waved wildly.

"We won! Yay, Dad!" Austin yelled as he leapt from his seat.

All over the stands, fans clapped and cheered. Kyle smiled and waved while *Mello Yello* circled the track.

Television and radio reporters rushed up to Kyle in Victory Lane.

"Way to go, Dad!" Austin said.
"You're the best driver and the best dad!"

When the three were ready to head home,
Austin shouted, "Race you to the car!" Kyle,
Austin, and Brice laughed as they tore across
the parking lot.